Book 1
CompTIA A+
By Solis Tech

&

Book 2
Open Source
By Solis Tech

Book 1
CompTIA A+
By Solis Tech

All-in-One Certification Exam Guide for Beginners!

Table Of Contents

Introduction

I want to thank you and congratulate you for purchasing the book, *"CompTIA A+: All-in-One Certification Exam Guide for Beginners!"*

This book contains proven steps and strategies on how to prepare for the CompTIA A+ exams.

This eBook will explain the basics of the CompTIA A+ certification and tests. It will also give you some pointers regarding the topics that you need to review. By reading this book, you will gain the knowledge and skills required to pass the tests.

Thanks again for purchasing this book, I hope you enjoy it!

Chapter 1: The CompTIA A+ Examination

This eBook is written for people who are knowledgeable about computers. It assumes that you know to how to use a computer and its peripherals (e.g. printers, modems, etc.). This book will serve as your guide in preparing for the CompTIA A+ exam.

The A+ Certification

This is a certification program developed by CompTIA (Computer Technology Industry Association). This program is designed to provide a consistent way of checking the competency of computer technicians. The A+ certificate is given to people who have reached the degree of knowledge and diagnostic skills required to give proper support in the PC industry.

The A+ certification is similar to other programs in the industry (e.g. Microsoft Certified Systems Engineer and Novell's Certified Novel Engineer). The principle behind these certification programs is that if you need to get services for their products, you want to find technicians who have been certified by these programs.

The Benefits of Being A+ Certified

There are many reasons to get your own A+ certification. The information packet distributed by CompTIA gives the following benefits:

- It serves as a proof of your professional achievement.

- It improves your marketability.

- It gives you excellent advancement opportunities.

- It is now considered as a requirement for other kinds of advanced computer training.

- It encourages customers to do business with you

How to Become Certified

The A+ certification is given to anyone who passes the exams. You are not required to work for any company. CompTIA is not a secret group or society. It is, on the other hand, a group of elite computer technicians. If you want to be A+ certified, you have to do these things:

- Pass the exam called A+ Essentials

- Pass one of the three technician examinations:

- o IT Technician Test
- o Depot Technician Test
- o Remote Support Technician Test

You can take the tests at any Pearson VUE or Thompson Prometric testing center. If you will pass both exams, you will receive a mail from CompTIA. That letter will inform you that you passed the tests. Additionally, it contains the certificate, a lapel pin, and a business card.

How to Sign Up for the Exams

To sign up for the tests, you may call Pearson VUE at 1-877-551-7587 or register online at www.vue.com. For Thompson Prometric, call 1-800-777-4276 or visit the website www.2test.com.

These companies will ask for your name, employer, phone number, mailing address, and SSN (Social Security Number). If you don't want to give out your SSN, a provisional number will be given to you. Additionally, they will ask when and where you want to take the exam.

Obviously, the exams aren't free. You have to pay your chosen testing company. That means you have to specify the payment arrangement during the registration process. You can simply provide your credit card information to the customer representative you will talk to. If you're doing it online, you can enter the credit card info on their payment page.

Who Should Use This Book?

If you want to pass the A+ tests, and do it confidently, you should use this book as a guide for your preparations. The A+ Essentials test is created to measure basic skills for an entry-level computer technician. The technician tests are designed to certify that you have the required skills to service microcomputer hardware.

This eBook was created with one purpose in mind: to help you pass the A+ exams. This guide will do that by explaining the things on which you will be tested.

Chapter 2: The Different Parts of a Computer

A PC (i.e. personal computer) is a machine made up of different components that work together to perform tasks (e.g. helping you write a document or add up large numbers). With this definition, notice that computers are described as having various distinct parts that work together harmoniously. Nowadays, almost all computers are modular. That is, they possess parts that can be replaced if the owner wants to improve the performance of his device. Each part has a specific purpose. In this chapter, you'll learn about the parts that make up a common PC, how they work, and what their functions are.

Important Note: Unless stated otherwise, the terms "computer" and "PC" can be used interchangeably throughout this eBook.

The Different Parts of a Motherboard

The motherboard, also called the system or planar board, serves as the "spine" of a PC. This is the brown or green circuit board that you'll find at the bottom of your computer. The system board is the most important part of a PC since it houses and/or connects the other parts of a computer together.

Different Types of Motherboards

There are two main types of motherboards. These are:

Integrated Motherboards – With this type, most of the parts are integrated into the system board's circuitry. Basically, integrated motherboards are created for simplicity. Since majority of the components are already part of the board itself, you won't have to install them individually. However, this simplicity has a major drawback: once a component stops working, you cannot simply replace it; you have to replace the entire motherboard. These boards are cheap to manufacture but expensive to repair.

Note: If one of the parts breaks, you may just disable it and add an expansion card that has similar capabilities.

Nonintegrated Motherboards – Here, the major parts (e.g. disk controllers, video circuitry, etc.) are installed as expansion cards. You will easily identify this kind of system board since every expansion slot is occupied by a major component.

The Different Form Factors of Motherboards

Computer experts also classify motherboards according to their design (also known as *form factor*). Here are the main form factors being used today: NLX, BTX, ATX, and micro ATX. You have to be vigilant when buying a computer case and system board separately. Some cases lack flexibility: they might not accommodate the system board you will select.

Let's discuss each form factor:

1. NLX – This is the abbreviation for "New Low-profile Extended". In general, this form factor is used for cases that are low-profile. With this design, the expansion slots (e.g. PCI, ISA, etc.) are placed on a special card to reduce the vertical space they occupy. Daughter boards, or adapter cards, that are normally plugged vertically into the expansion slots, are placed parallel to the system board. That means their size won't affect that of the computer case.

2. BTX – This form factor was launched by Intel back in 2003. With this design, the head-producing parts are lined up against the power supply's exhaust fan and the air intake vents. Then, the other components are cooled by installing heat sinks on the motherboard. This design offers a quiet setup since it involves efficient airflow paths and fewer exhaust fans.

3. ATX – With ATX motherboards, the processor and memory slots form a 90° angle with the expansion cards. This design places the memory and processor in line with the power supply's exhaust fan. Thus, the processor can remain cool while it runs. In addition, you may add expansion cards (even the full-length ones) to an ATX motherboard since the memory and processor are not parallel to the expansion cards.

4. Micro ATX – This form factor is similar with the previous one, with one major difference: it is designed for smaller computer cases. Micro ATX motherboards benefit from the enhanced cooling designs of their full-sized counterparts. However, since they are smaller, they have lesser motherboard headers, integrated components, expansion slots, and memory modules.

Processors – Their Functions and Characteristics

Now that you are familiar with system boards, you have to learn about their most important part: the central processing unit (CPU). The CPU controls all of the computer's activities using both internal and external buses. Basically, it is a processor chip that contains millions of transistors.

Important Note: Nowadays, the word "chip" describes the whole package that a computer technician may install into a socket. However, this word was originally used to refer to the silicon wafer hidden inside the carrier (i.e. the "chip" you see on your motherboard). The pins that you see on the outer part of the carrier are connected to the silicon wafer's small contacts. These pins allow you to install the carrier into a socket.

You can identify which part inside the PC is the central processing unit: the CPU is a large square that lies flat on the motherboard with a large fan and heat sink.

The Features of Modern Processors

- Hyperthreading – This word refers to HTT (hyper-threading technology). Basically, HTT is a variant of SMT (simultaneous multithreading). This kind of technology uses the scalar architecture of modern CPUs.

  HTT-capable CPUs appear as two different processors to the computer's operating system (OS). Because of this, the OS may assign two processes simultaneously, such as symmetric multi-processing, where multiple processors utilize the same network resources. Actually, the OS should support SMP in order to use HTT. If a process fails because of missing information caused by, for instance, branch prediction problems, the processor's execution resources can be reassigned for a different procedure that can be conducted immediately. Thus, the processor's downtime is dramatically reduced.

- Multicore – A CPU that has a multicore design contains two processors inside the same package. Here, the OS may treat the CPU as if it were two different CPUs. Just like the HTT, the OS should support SMP. Additionally, SMP is not considered as an upgrade if the apps run on the SMP system are not meant for parallel processes. A good example for the multicore technology is the i7 Quad-Core Processor from Intel.

- Microcode – This is the group of instructions (also called instruction set) that compose the different microprograms that the CPU executes as it performs its functions. The MMX (multimedia extensions) is a special example of an individual microprogram that performs a specific instruction set. Basically, microcodes are at a lower level than the codes used in computer programs. On average, each instruction from a computer program requires a large number of microinstructions. Intel and other processor manufacturers incorporate the MMX instruction set into their products.

- Overclocking – This feature allows you to increase the performance of your CPU, on par with processors created to function at overclocked rates. However, unlike processors created to function on that speed, you have to make sure that the overclocked processor doesn't damage itself from the increased level of heat. You might need to install an advanced cooling system (e.g. liquid cooling) to protect the CPU and other computer parts.

- Throttling – Processor throttling, also called clamping, is the process that specifies the CPU time to be spent on a computer program. By specifying how individual programs use the processor, you can "treat" all of the applications fairly. The principle of Application Fairness turns into a major problem for servers, where each program may represent the work of another user. That means fairness to computer programs becomes fairness to the users (i.e. the actual customers). Customers of modern terminal servers take advantage of this feature.

Memory – Its Functions and Characteristics

Nowadays, memory is one of the easy, popular, and inexpensive methods to enhance a computer. While the computer's processor runs, it stores data in the machine's memory. Basically, the more memory a machine has, the faster it can operate.

To determine the memory of a computer, search for thin sets of small circuit boards that are packed together near the CPU. These circuit boards sit vertically on the computer's motherboard.

How to Check for Errors in a Computer's Memory

Parity Checking

This is a basic scheme used to check for errors. It lines up the computer chips in a single column and separates them into equal bit groups. These bits are numbered beginning at zero. All of the number x bits, one from every chip, create a numerical array. If you are using "even parity", for instance, you will count up the number of bits contained in the array. If the total number is even, you will set the parity bit to zero since the bit count is already even. If the total is an odd number, on the other hand, you should set the parity bit to 1 in order to even up the bit count.

This technique is effective in identifying the existence of errors in the arrays of bits. However, it cannot indicate the location of the errors and how to solve them. Keep in mind that this isn't error correction – it is just a simple error check.

ECC

ECC stands for *Error Checking and Correcting*. If the computer's memory supports this method, the system will generate and store check bits. Whenever the machine accesses its memory, an algorithm will be performed on the check bits. If the result turns out to be zero (or a group of zeros), the information contained in the memory is considered valid and the computer functions as normal. ECC can identify single-bit and double-bit errors. However, it can only correct errors that are single-bit in nature.

The Four Main Types of Memory

- **DRAM** – This is perhaps the most popular type of RAM out there. DRAM stands for *Dynamic Random Access Memory*. Because of their inherent simplicity, these memory chips are cheap and easy to create compared to the other types. This kind of memory is called dynamic since it needs constant update signals in order to keep storing the data written there. If the DRAM chips won't receive stable signals, the information they hold will be deleted.

- **SRAM** – This stands for *Static Random Access Memory*. Unlike DRAMs, this kind of memory doesn't require a steady stream of signals. In general, SRAM chips are more complex and expensive than DRAMs. You can use SRAM for cache functions.

- **ROM** – This is the abbreviation for Read-Only Memory. It is called as such because it prevents the user from editing the memory it contains. Once the data is written on the computer's ROM, it cannot be changed anymore. ROM is usually used to hold the machine's BIOS, since this data is rarely modified.

- **CMOS** – This is a special type of memory chip. It is designed to hold the configuration settings of a computer's BIOS. CMOS is battery-powered: that means the configuration is retained even if the machine is turned off.

Storage Devices – Their Functions and Characteristics

Computers are useless if they can't store anything. Storage devices hold the information being used, as well as the programs and files the computer needs in order to function properly. In general, storage devices are classified according to their capacity, access time, and physical attributes.

HDD Systems

HDD stands for *Hard Disk Drive*. This storage device is also called hard disk or hard drive. Computers use HDDs to allow quick access to data as well as permanent storage. Typically, hard disks are found inside a computer.

An HDD system is composed of:

Controller – This component controls the storage. It knows how the drive functions, emits signals to the different motors inside the disk, and accepts signals from the sensors within the drive. Nowadays, hard disk manufacturers place the drive and controller in one enclosure.

Hard Disk – This acts as the physical warehouse for the data. HDD systems store data on little disks (about 3-5 inches in diameter) grouped together and kept inside an enclosure.

Host Adapter – This is the system's translator: it converts signals from the controller and hard disk to signals the computer can work with. Most modern motherboards have a built-in host adapter, allowing drive cable connection through board headers.

Floppy Drives

Floppy disks are magnetic storage devices that use plastic diskettes enclosed in a tough casing. Several years ago, floppy disks were used to easily transfer information from one computer to another. Nowadays, few people are using floppy disks because of their small capacity. DVD-ROMs and CD-ROMs have replaced floppy disks in storing and transferring digital information.

CD-ROM Drives

Modern computers use CD-ROM drives. These compact disks are virtually similar to those used in music recording. CD-ROMs allow you to store data for a long period of time. In general, these drives are read-only: you cannot erase or delete the data once it is stored on a CD. In addition, computers need to spend a longer time in "reading" CDs compared to internal hard drives. Why are these drives so popular?

Despite their drawbacks, CD-ROMs are used because they can store large files (about 650MB) and are extremely portable.

DVD-ROM Drives

This is the newest storage device to be used for computers. The DVD (i.e. digital video disc) technology is mostly used for entertainment purposes (e.g. home theater systems). DVD-ROMs are basically similar to the DVDs you use at home. Because of this, computers that are equipped with a DVD-ROM drive can play movies stored on a DVD.

However, DVD-ROMs are way much more useful when used for computers. Since they use newer technology, DVD-ROMs are better than CD-ROMs in terms of storage capacity. On average, DVDs can hold 4GB of data. That means DVD-ROMs are your best option if you are storing or distributing large files.

Important Note: CD-ROMs and DVD-ROMs have the same appearance. The single difference is the logo on the front of DVD drives.

Removable Storage Devices

Many years ago, the term "removable storage" meant something extremely different from what it means now. Tape backup is one of the old storage devices that can still be bought today. Modern computer users prefer the solid-state, random-access removable storage devices. In this section, you'll learn about tape backups and the new storage solutions.

Tape Backup

This is an old type of removable storage. A tape backup device can be installed externally or internally and utilize either an analog or digital magnetic tape to store data. In general, this kind of device can hold more information than other storage mediums. However, they are also one of the slowest in terms of data transfer rate. Because of these reasons, tape backup devices are mainly used for archived information.

Flash Memory

Before, random-access memory chips were only used to access and use data. But now, you'll find them in different physical sizes and storage capacities. Flash memory drives are considered as the best solid-state storage device available. The flash memory category includes SD (secure digital) and other memory cards, USB flash drives, and older detachable and non-detachable memory mechanisms. Each of these storage devices has the capability to store huge amounts of information.

Manufacturers of flash memory devices use revolutionary packaging (e.g. keychain attachments) for their products to provide easy transport options for their end-users.

Chapter 3: How to Work With Computer Parts Effectively

While taking the CompTIA A+ exam, you will answer questions regarding the installation, usage, and replacement of computer parts. This chapter will help you to review regarding those topics.

How to Install, Configure and Optimize Computer Parts

Aside from knowing the characteristics and functions of PC components, you also need to know how to use them. In particular, you should be familiar with the installation, configuration, and optimization of such parts.

How to Upgrade a Storage Device

Storage devices are available in different shapes and sizes. Aside from IDE and SCSI, two of the most popular types, there are SATA (Serial ATA) and PATA (Parallel ATA). You can also   differentiate between external and internal drives. This section of the book will explain each of these options.

Preparing the Drive

Regardless of the technology being used, you should format storage devices before using them. Although most drives have their own formatting software, each OS has a tool that you can use. When working with Windows computers, you can utilize the format utility through the command line. If you are working with XP, Vista, 7, or newer Windows system, you can also use the graphical utility program called Disk Management.

How to Work with IDE

Before, IDE (integrated drive electronics) drives were the most popular kind of computer hard drives. Although they are often linked to hard drives, IDE is more than just an interface for hard disks. It can also serve as the interface for different storage types such as Zip, DVD, and CD-ROM.

To install IDE drives, you should:

1. Set the slave/master jumper on the IDE drive.

2. Place the drive inside the drive bay.

3. Connect the cable for power-supply.

4. Link the ribbon cable to the motherboard and to the drive.

5. If the drive isn't detected automatically, you should configure it using the BIOS Setup of your computer.

6. Use your PC's operating system to format and partition the IDE drive.

How to Work with SCSI

SCSI is the abbreviation for *Small Computer System Interface*. This kind of device can be either external or internal to the machine. To configure an SCSI device, you should assign an SCSI ID (also called SCSI address) to all of the devices in the SCSI bus. You can configure their numbers using a jumper or DIP switch.

Whenever the computer sends data to the SCSI device, it emits a signal on the cable assigned to that number. The device will respond with a signal that holds the device's number and the information needed.

You should install a terminator (i.e. terminating resistor device) at the two ends of the bus to keep the SCSI devices working. You can activate and/or deactivate terminators using a jumper.

Here are the things you should do when installing an SCSI device:

- For Internal Devices – Connect the cable (i.e. a 50-wire ribbon cable with multiple keyed connectors) to the adapter and to each SCSI device in your computer. Afterward, place the terminators on the adapter and terminate the final device in the chain. You should leave other devices unterminated.

- For External Devices - Follow the steps outlined above, but here, you should use some stub cables between the SCSI devices in the daisy chain (instead of a long cable that has multiple connectors). Terminate the adapter as well as the final device in the daisy chain (that device should have one stub cable linked to it).

- For Hybrid Devices – Many types of adapters have connectors for external and internal SCSI devices. If you have this kind of adapter, attach the ribbon cable to your internal devices and connect the cable to your adapter. Afterward, daisy-chain the external devices from the external port. Terminate the device at the end of every chain. Make sure that the adapter is unterminated.

External Storage Devices

As capacities shoot up and prices fall down, the number of available external storage devices has increased greatly. Aside from the SCSI variant explained above, you will also see devices with USB connections and those that can connect straight to the system. The computer's operating system will recognize USB devices upon connection. You can just install any additional programs you like to use. A computer program called Dantz Retrospect is included in many storage devices to allow you to utilize external devices as automatic backups.

If the external storage device is linked straight to the system, you can just follow the instructions that came with that product. Then, install additional programs on the computers that you will be using. The main benefit of linking straight to the system is that the storage device/s can be accessed by all of the computers.

How to Upgrade Display Devices

Before linking or unlinking a display device (e.g. a computer monitor), make sure that the computer and the device itself are powered off. Afterward, connect a cable from the computer's video card to the display device. Connect the power cord of that device to an electrical outlet. You may use a modern Digital Visual Interface (DVI) cable or the traditional DB-15 (or VGA) cable.

While installing a new monitor, you should have the proper driver. The driver is the software interface between the display device and the computer's OS. If you don't have the right driver, your monitor won't display what you want to see. Nowadays, you can download the newest drivers from the website of monitor manufacturers.

Aside from the power supply, the most dangerous part to repair is the monitor. Computer technicians say that beginners should never attempt to repair monitors. Monitors can hold high-voltage charges even if they have been powered off for several hours. That means you can be electrocuted if you will try to repair a monitor by yourself. If your monitor stopped working, and you don't want to buy a new one, you should take that device to a TV repair shop or a certified computer technician. The technicians and the repair guys know how to fix monitors properly – they understand the dangers and the correct procedures.

How to upgrade Input and Multimedia Devices

The typical upgrade for input devices is the transition to newer mice and keyboards.

Keyboards

Keyboards may wear out if used repeatedly. The usual problem is "key sticking", where keys are no longer responding to the user. To replace a PS/2 101-key keyboard with a new one, just unplug the old keyboard and plug in the new. As you can see, this is a quick and easy process. Nowadays, however, computer users prefer to replace old keyboards with USB ones.

Here is a principle you need to remember: You can use the "unplug-the-old-and-plug-in-the-new" procedure as long as your computer's OS supports the keyboard you want to use.

Mice

Computer mice also wear out because of repeated use. But don't worry: you can replace old mice with new ones. You may easily replace a PS/2 connection mouse with another without spending too much. As an alternative, you may buy an optical mouse (which prevents dust- and ball-related problems) or a wireless one (which needs batteries to send and receive signals). Although new mouse models still use the PS/2 type of connection, most mouse products in the market use the USB connection.

Chapter 4: The Tools Needed for Checking Computer Parts

The CompTIA A+ exam will also test your skills in checking computer parts. This chapter will help you with that topic by discussing the tools and diagnostic procedures needed.

The Tools Needed by a Computer Technician

A great computer technician needs a great collection of tools. If you are working alone, you may not get past the troubleshooting phase. However, you still need to use certain tools in order to succeed in that task. Once you have identified the problem, you will need to get another set of tools in order to fix it.

This book will focus on the "hardware" tools. These are:

- Screwdrivers – When checking a computer technician's toolkit, you will surely find screwdrivers. Almost all of the big computer parts you'll see today are mounted using screws. If you need to remove these parts, you need to have the right type of screwdriver. This kind of tool is divided into three types:

    o Flat-Blade – Many people refer to this as the *common* or *standard* screwdriver. The screw used with this screwdriver is rarely used today (mainly because the screw's head can be destroyed easily).

    o Phillips – This is perhaps the most popular type of screwdrivers being used today. The screws used with a Phillips screwdriver have enough head surface: you can turn them many times without damaging the screws' head. According to recent reports, more than 90% of the screws used in computers belong to the Phillips-head type.

    o Torx – This is the type of screwdriver you use while working on tiny screws found on Apple and Compaq computers. The screws you remove using a Torx screwdriver have the most surface to work against: they offer the best resistance in terms of screw-head damage. Nowadays, Torx-type screws are gaining more popularity because of their clean and technical look.

- Flashlight – This is one of the tools you should always have. You'll realize how important this tool is when you're crawling under a table searching for a dropped computer part.

19

- Needle-Nose Pliers – You should have this in your toolkit. This kind of pliers is great for holding connectors or tiny screws (particularly if you have large hands). If needle-nose pliers are still too big to do certain tasks, you may use a pair of tweezers.

- Compressed Air – While working on a computer, you will usually remove the machine's case first. Once the cover is removed, it would be great if you will clean the computer's internal components. The clumps of dirt and fibers can block airflow inside the system unit. As a result, the PC's life will be shortened. The ideal way to eliminate the dust is by using compressed air.

  If you are working for a big company, you probably have a core air compressor that supplies compressed air. If this kind of compressor is not available, you may purchase canned compressed air. However, you'll be shelling out large amounts of money – cans of compressed air are expensive.

- Soldering Iron – You can use it to splice broken wires. Nowadays, computer technicians rarely use this tool. Here's the reason: modern computer parts are created with quick-disconnect connectors. You can easily replace them without splicing anything.

- Wire Strippers – Whenever you have to solder something, you need to use a stripper/wire cutter to prepare the wires for connection. Stripping means you will expose a certain part of the wire by removing the insulation.

- Multi-Meters – This tool is named as such because it is basically a set of different types of testing meters, such as ammeter, voltmeter, and ohmmeter. When used by a trained technician, a multi-meter can identify the failure of various types of computer parts.

  A multi-meter has an analog or digital display, a mode selector switch, and two probes. You can use the switch to perform two things: (1) select the function you want to test and (2) choose the range in which the meter will work. If you need to use an old meter to measure a power pack, you should manually set the range selector. Modern multi-meters, particularly the digital ones, can automatically find the correct ranges.

  Important Note: You should never measure voltage by connecting a manual ranging multi-meter to an AC electrical outlet. This will damage the meter itself, the meter mechanisms, or both.

  <u>How to Measure Resistance Using a Multi-Meter</u>

Resistance is the property of electricity commonly measured when troubleshooting computer parts. This electrical property is measured in ohms and represented by the Greek letter "omega." If a multi-meter indicates infinite resistance, the electric currents cannot travel from one prove to another. If you are using a multi-meter to check the resistance and you are getting an infinite reading, there's a huge possibility that the wire is broken.

When measuring resistance, you should set the tool to measure ohms. You can do it using either the selector dial or the front button. Then, connect the PC component you want to measure between the tool's probes. The multi-meter will then show the component's resistance value.

How to Measure Voltage Using a Multi-Meter

This process is similar to the one discussed above, but with two main differences:

1. While measuring voltage, make sure that you properly connect each probe to the source of electricity. For DC voltage, the "-" should be connected to the negative side and the "+" to the positive one. This positioning is irrelevant when measuring AC voltage.

2. You should switch the selector to Volts DC (VDC) or Volts AC (VAC), depending on what you need to measure, to instruct the tool about the voltage you are working with. These settings protect the tool from overload. The multi-meter will blow up if you will plug it into a power source while it's still on "measure resistance" mode.

Chapter 5: Operating Systems

The CompTIA A+ examination will test your knowledge regarding operating systems. Since operating systems play an important role in the computer industry, you should be familiar with them. This chapter will guide you in this topic. Here, you'll learn different things about a computer's OS.

What is an Operating System?

Computers are useless if they don't have any piece of software. Well, you can use them as a doorstop or paperweight – but that is not cost-efficient. You need to have an interface before you can use the capabilities of a computer. And, if you don't know yet, software acts as the interface. Although there are different kinds of software, or computer programs, the most important one you'll ever need is the OS.

Operating systems have various functions, most of which are extremely complex. However, two functions are critical:

1. Interfacing with the computer's hardware

2. Providing an environment in which other pieces of software can run.

Here are the three main types of software that you will encounter in the CompTIA exam:

- Operating System – It provides a stable environment for other computer programs. In addition, it allows the user to enter and execute commands. The operating system gives the user an interface so they can enter commands (i.e. input) and get results or feedback (i.e. output). For this, the OS should communicate with the PC's hardware and conduct the tasks below:

    o Device access

    o Output format

    o Memory management

    o File and disk management

Once the operating system has performed these basic tasks, the user can enter instructions to the computer using an input device (e.g. a mouse or keyboard). Some of the commands are pre-installed in the operating system, whereas others are given using certain applications. The OS serves as the platform on which the PC's hardware, other pieces of software, and the user work together.

- Application – This is used to complete a specific task. Basically, an application is a computer program written to support the commands given to the OS. Every application is compiled or configured for the operating system it will be used for. Because of this, the application depends on the OS to perform most of its basic functions.

  When a program accesses the computer's memory and linked devices, it sends a request to the OS. The machine's operating system will perform the requests made by the program being used. This setup helps greatly in decreasing the programming overhead, since most of the executable codes are shared – they are written onto the operating system and can be used by different applications installed on the computer.

- Driver – This is an extremely specific program created to instruct an operating system on how to access and use a piece of hardware (e.g. webcam, flash memory, etc.). Every webcam or flash memory has distinct features and settings – the driver helps the OS in knowing how the new hardware works and the things it can do.

The Terms and Concepts Related to Operating Systems

In this section, let's define some of the most important terms and concepts. Study this section carefully since it will teach you the terms you'll encounter during the CompTIA A+ exam.

Key Terms

- Source – This is the code that explains how computer programs work. An operating system can be open source or closed source.

  - Open Source – The users have the right to change and examine the code.

  - Closed Source – The users are not allowed to edit or check the code.

- Version – This is a specific variant of a computer program, usually expressed by a number, which informs users regarding the "newness" of the software. For instance, MS-DOS is now in its sixth main version. Computer programmers distinguish minor revisions from major ones this way:

  - "Program" 4.0 to "Program" 5.0 is a major revision.

  - "Program" 5.0 to "Program" 5.2 is a minor revision.

- Shell – A piece of software that works on top of the operating system. It allows users to execute commands through an array of menus or a different type of graphical interface. A shell makes an operating system simpler and easier to use by modifying the GUI (graphical user interface).

- GUI – The method by which a user communicates with computers. A GUI uses a touchpad, mouse, or a different mechanism (aside from a keyboard) to interact with the machine and issue commands.

- Multithreading – The capability of a computer program to contain several requests in the computer's CPU. Since it allows an application to perform different tasks simultaneously, computers experience a boost in performance and efficiency.

- Network – A group of computers that are connected by a communication link. A network allows computers to share resources and information.

- Preemptive Multitasking – This is a multitasking technique in which the operating system allocates each program a certain amount of CPU time. Afterward, the OS takes back the control and provides another task or program access to the CPU. Basically, if a computer program crashes, the operating system takes the processor from the faulty program and gives it to the next one (which must be working). Even though unstable computer programs still get locked, only the affected application will stop – not the whole machine.

- Cooperative Multitasking – This is a multitasking technique that relies on the applications themselves. Here, each program is responsible for utilizing and giving up access to the CPU. Windows 3.1 used this method to manage multiple programs. If an application stalls while it is using the CPU, the application fails to free the CPU properly, and the whole computer gets locked, the user needs to reboot the machine.

Conclusion

Thank you again for purchasing this book!

I hope this book was able to help you to prepare for the CompTIA A+ tests.

The next step is to reread this book and use other information sources. That way, you can increase your chances of passing the exam.

Finally, if you enjoyed this book, please take the time to share your thoughts and post a review on Amazon. It'd be greatly appreciated!

Thank you and good luck!

Book 2
Open Source
By Solis Tech

Understanding Open Source From the Beginning!

Open Source: Understanding Open Source From the Beginning!

Table Of Contents

Introduction

I want to thank you and congratulate you for purchasing the book, *"Open Source: Understanding Open Source From the Beginning!"*

This book contains the basics in understanding the open source concept. What is it all about? Where did it come from? Who creates the open source content? How can software be considered as an 'open source'? What makes it different from the other software that we already have?

These questions are answered in this book. Also included in this book are information relevant to open source, such as examples of licensing, the Four Freedoms of free software use, and ideas about software piracy. This information will help to further understand what it means to have some software that is open sourced.

Real life comparisons are also made in this book in case you become confused or lost in understanding the open source concept. The idea of open source seems very simple, but in reality, it is very complex, with definitions coinciding with the definitions of other concepts such as free software (which will further be discussed in Chapter Two). Listed down in the book are the advantages and disadvantages of open source software, and the reasons why more and more people are becoming enticed with the idea of converting to open source.

If the present generation already dictates the movement of open source software, what will become of it in the future? This question is also answered in the last chapter of this book. Due to the fast-paced advancement of technology, open source will adapt to this advancement with the help of both developers and users.

Thanks again for purchasing this book, I hope you enjoy it!

Chapter 1: The Basics of Open Source

Have you ever wondered how an application you're using works? Every time you use an application and it freezes, do you think about what could have gone wrong? Do you ever think of why applications are constantly updating? These are questions that you would not be asked often. But these questions are very important to you, as a user of the Internet age.

Application programs are comprised of source codes, and these source codes are made by programmers. These codes are what allow you to type words into a word processing document, or to click on that video of cats meowing simultaneously. What you see onscreen are only visual representations of the codes of the program. Your application programs may be paid, or pre-installed in your devices, so you don't have permission to view these codes. Rather, you get the pre-made product, and you as a consumer have no power over it except to use it as instructed.

When you purchase or download an application and place it in your device, it installs a lot of files, but none of these files contain the source code. A software manager is included in your installed files to monitor the application as you use it. Whenever your application gets bugged or freezes, this software manager runs, and it prompts you to file a report to the software's developers to tell them exactly what happened. Once the report is filed, the developers study the bug, fix it, and release an update a few days or weeks later.

But what if you could see these codes for yourself? What if, whenever something goes wrong with the application, you could easily contact the developers or ask for help from other programmers easily? These questions are the foundations of open source, and you are about to learn more about it in the following chapters.

What is Open Source?

Open source is a computer program that has its source code visible to the public. The public – which we can refer to as the users – have the power to view, copy, and modify the source codes to their liking. The source code and the compiled version of the code are distributed freely to the users without fixed fees. Users of open source can pretty much do anything they like with the open source programs that they downloaded, since there are practically no restrictions.

To better understand the concept of open source software, let us use an example of recipes for comparison.

Recipes start off with someone writing them down on a piece of paper. A grandma, perhaps, has a recipe for a cake, which she writes in her recipe book. She passes on this recipe to her children, and tells them that they can use the recipe whenever they like. But, they must make sure to credit her as the original creator of the recipe.

The children recreate the recipe and whenever they are asked where the recipe is from, they would always tell that it's from grandma. One of grandma's children alters the cake recipe by adding strawberries as an extra ingredient. The grandma allows this, given that she is also permitted to use the altered recipe.

This example has the same concept with open source software.

When a programmer writes a code, compiles it into a program, and distributes both the source code and the compiled program to the users, he is giving everyone permission to access everything about the program. Users can run the program, view the code, modify if needed, compile, and redistribute the modified version of the program.

The original programmer, however, would require the users to let him use the modified versions of his program, since it is his to begin with. Aside from this certain restriction, the users of the program have the freedom to do whatever they like to do with it.

Let's go back to the example of the cake recipe. One of grandma's children, the one who added the strawberries, suggests to grandma to add the strawberries to the original recipe. The grandma thinks that this is a good idea therefore she complies and replaces her old recipe with the altered cake recipe.

In open source software, if the programmer is notified of a certain modification of a user, and it is deemed to be a modification that the software needs, then the programmer will revise his program based on that certain modification. This modification is called a patch. The user who has suggested of the modification is now coined as a contributor. This process of adapting user modification to an open source software is called upstreaming, because the modification goes back to the original code.

The concept of open source depends on the communication and collaboration between the software's developers and its users. Bug detection and fixing of open source is made easier because numerous users are working simultaneously to study the source code and to compile a modified, fixed version of the code.

With open source, it is not only the developers who are finding new ways on how the software can be improved and upgraded. The users can also contribute their ideas and knowledge in the upgrading of the software. The original developer or programmer can be called the maintainer who monitors the changes in his or her original software.

Let us then go back to the cake recipe. What if another child of grandma decides to do his own version of the cake recipe? He adds raisins to the cake recipe, and asks grandma if the raisins can be added with the strawberries in the original recipe. Grandma refuses, because she dislikes raisins. Instead of being disheartened, this child decides that he would create his own version of the recipe and share it with the people he knows.

If a certain modification makes no appeal to the developer, the one who suggested the modification may opt to make his own version of the program. This act of not patching a modification from the original program is called forking. A forked program is a certain program that alters the original program in such a way that it becomes its own program.

A forked program can be described as a chip off an old block, since it doesn't necessarily separate itself from the license of the program it originated from, although it may seem like it due to the avoidance of patching. Programmers that collaborate with open source result to forking if their modified versions of the original program are deemed unfit by the program's developer.

Nonprofit organizations are the prime developers of open source software. However, due to the freedom of customization that open source has given both users and developers, even large companies are adhering to the open source culture.

How did Open Source become popular?

During the early times of computing, software followed a protocol and design with everyone conforming to a certain cookie-cutter ideal. Software was yet to be imagined as cost-free, and the developers kept their codes to themselves. But then, during the early 90's, the idea of sharing one's code to the public became an accepted idea to most users. The concept of software being free and open sourced became a reality when, after decades, the likes of Mozilla Firefox and OpenOffice were created.

Open source rose in its ranks when developers started making open source alternatives of commercial software. These alternatives are free and can easily be downloaded from the internet, enticing most users to convert to open source. What made open source rise, however, was the idea of community. Fellow programmers could interact and communicate with each other, and even with the developers, which was unheard of during the early times of computing. People could collaborate with the developers of the software and share their insights.

Open source has also given its users the freedom to fully inspect software before they use it – an action that was impossible to do with closed source software. Users who are into coding try open source and study the code line by line.

The popularity of open source software has been anticipated due to the fact that a lot of people supported the cause. Programmers started creating open source projects to contribute to the cause, and users started to get accustomed to obtaining and downloading open source software. With volunteers signing up left and right, and organizations creating their own programs, the growth and expansion of open source software cannot be stopped anymore.

Chapter 2: History, Comparisons, and Relevance

Open source was not immediately implemented until the early 90's, where more and more people began to realize the importance of being able to share the source code of software without fees and royalties. Like any other idea, open source started out as a small thought of making software free for the public, and grew into the culture that it is today.

The History of Open Source: The Open Source Initiative

Eric Raymond, an American software developer, published an essay (turned book) entitled The Cathedral and the Bazaar in 1997. The essay speaks about two different types of software, which he labels the Cathedral and the Bazaar.

In the essay, Raymond describes the Cathedral to be the type of software in which with each release of software, the source code of the software will be available. However, with each build of the software, the certain code block that has been modified is restricted to only the developers of the software. The examples presented under the Cathedral type of software were GNU Emacs (a type of text editor) and the GNU Compiler Collection (a compiler that caters to different programming languages).

In contrast, the Bazaar is the type of software that has the Internet as the venue for their development, making the code visible to the public. The example presented under the Bazaar type of software was Linux (now a widely known computer operating system), in which Raymond coined the developer Linus Torvalds to be the creator of the Bazaar type of software.

Raymond's article became popular in 1998, getting the attention of major companies and fellow programmers. Netscape was influenced by this article, leading them to release the source codes of their internet suite called Netscape Communicator. The source code of the said internet suit was what gave birth to internet browsers such as Thunderbird and SeaMonkey. Mozilla Firefox, a popular web browser today, was also based from the source codes of Netscape Communicator.

The idea of source codes being free became widespread when Linux was developed, urging people to contribute to the open source cause. Because of the increasing popularity of Linux and similar projects, people who became interested in the cause formed the Open Source Initiative, a group whose advocacy is to tell people about the benefits of open sourcing and why it is needed in the computing world.

Open Source vs. Free Software

Most people confused open source software with free software, as the two terms share somewhat the same advocacy. With understanding, it is not that difficult to tell these two terms apart.

The difference between free software and open source software can be listed down into different points. Although they have their differences, both free software and open source software have a singular goal – to publicize source codes for the users to see.

Free software focuses mainly on the ethical aspect of the advocacy. There are certain freedoms that free software are fighting for when it comes to the use of software, which cannot be given to the users by commercial software. These are the Four Freedoms of software use according to advocates of free software:

•   The freedom to use the software. This means that the user is free to use the software to his or her needs, or as instructed.

•   The freedom to study the source codes of the software. Since the codes are readily available for public viewing, the user has the freedom to view and study the said codes. After he or she reviews the codes, he or she then has the freedom to do the next step.

•   The freedom to modify the source codes of the software to the user's liking. If necessary, the user has the freedom to customize the source code and to create a version of the program fit for the user's specific needs.

•   The freedom to share the modified, compiled source codes to the public. If the program has been modified, the user has the freedom to compile and publish the modified program for the benefit of the other users who may also have the need of the program's modification. The developer of the original program should also be given the freedom and right to use the modified version of the program.

Free software allows its users to do whatever they want with a program. If they want to modify the source code and redistribute the modified code as their own, without the consent of the original developers, then they are free to do so. If the user wishes to use the source code as the base code of a new project that they are working on, then they will not be sued. The ethical reasoning of free software simply states that there are no grave restrictions when it comes to copying, revising, and republishing the already existing software.

Open source, on the other hand, creates programs with the Four Freedoms in mind. The programs which are considered open source are made for the user's convenience and benefit. The common idea of open source is a group of people working on a single open source project, attempting to create a program that will be beneficial to them, as well as the users.

Open Source and Paid Software

Open source software did indeed come from paid software. There are countless of open source alternatives for common, commercially-sold software readily available on the internet. Some examples of this are office suites like LibreOffice and OpenOffice, which are open source alternatives for the much more popular Microsoft Office.

The reason why open source alternatives of paid software exist is mainly the cost. Users would opt to pay less, or none at all, for certain software. Why pay for software when there are free alternatives that can be downloaded from the internet easily? Open source makes it possible for users who cannot afford paid software to experience the basic and intermediate features of the software, without sacrificing the quality of the end product.

Although open source may be the overall solution for users to get a feel of certain software, there are still others who would want to obtain paid software but through illegal means. This is called software piracy, an action that is still evident despite it being illegal in most countries.

Software piracy is the act of downloading or installing a paid software illegally, either through software cracks or illegally burned CDs. The most popular way to obtain pirated software is through downloading Torrent-based software crack, in which the user can get the files through different computers almost discreetly. Since these software are pirated, installing these software requires the user to turn off his or her Internet connection before installing, to avoid being tracked.

Some paid software can be bought once, and shared with different computers or devices. All of the information regarding the sharing of paid software can be found on the software's End User License Agreement or EULA. The EULA is a splash screen shown at the start of the software's installation which contains the contract between the software's developers and the user.

The EULA may allow the user to share one copy of the software to different devices, or it may restrict the user from doing so. Once the user has violated this part of the EULA, it can then be considered as software piracy.

Something that a user should be aware of is a certain license called the GNU General Public License, the license that most open source software adhere to. The license permits the user to copy, modify, and redistribute the modified code, just as long as the source files and the original codes are still documented. This is important in understanding how and why open source software is allowed to move freely across the internet without being coined as software piracy, as compared to paid, propriety software.

With propriety or paid software, the user is buying only the license. He is not allowed to revise the code, to reverse-engineer the code, and to view the code by all means. The only thing that the user is allowed to do when he purchases propriety software is to use a copy of the software that the developer has provided. It may seem like an unfair deal to some people, because a user should be able to own something that he has paid for.

Open source software changes that idea. It gives the user the freedom to see the program's source code, letting the user know the program's 'skeletal system'. Even without paying for the software, the user gets the full potential functions of the software and not just an executable copy of it.

Importance of Open Source

Technology is rapidly changing. Experts are coming up with more ways to improve the lives of other people. It is the same with those who contribute to open source projects. Their advocacy is to create free programs that will benefit the users.

Open source is important in the evolution of quality software. With a lot of people contributing to one singular project, the software that is produced will be the best of its kind as it has been meticulously observed and reviewed by the contributors. Open source gives way for the collaborative effort of different programmers and users, with the users being secondary developers of a certain program. It is an interactive effort, with the users being able to update the program alongside the developers themselves.

The fast paced advancement of technology would often overwhelm content creators to the point that they would stop creating content altogether. Content creators who are left behind by technology's advancement are often working in small groups or on their own, and have no means of help from fellow creators of their kind.

With Open source, this is never the case. Each open source software has its own community to back a fellow programmer up during each build, ready to help out other programmers and users when needed. The open source community's bond with each other is what makes open source catch up with the fast advancement of technology.

Chapter 3: The Benefits and the Downsides of Open Source

The Benefits of Open Source

The most obvious perk of having open source software is the availability of the source code. With the source code available to the general public, people are able to study the code line by line. Students of programming can study the source code and implement some blocks of it into their own projects, honing their skills and improving their code. Users who are meticulous with their software can view the codes and customize the said codes to their liking.

Aside from the source codes being publicized, another perk of having open source software is that it is mostly free, depending on the software's license. Users of open source software do not have to pay a large sum of money to be able to enjoy the full functions of the software. If the license requires the user to pay, the user may still try out the software's full functions before purchasing.

Open source promotes community. If a user encounters a problem with the downloaded software, he or she can seek help from fellow programmers or the developers themselves through a forum. Users and programmers alike can communicate and share their experiences with using the software, helping other users to get used to the software. With other programmers keen on editing and revising the source code, updated and better versions of the software can easily be uploaded and shared within the community for the benefit of the other users.

Also, when something goes wrong with the open source software, the user has the option to fix the problem himself should seeking help be an option that is not convenient for him. In propriety software, this cannot be possible as the license and copyright prohibits its users from ever touching the program's source code.

If the user of propriety software does as much as reverse-engineer the product, then they could be violating the program's copyright and therefore, be taken to jail. Open source software removes this restriction from the users, giving them permission to fix solvable program problems on their own.

The benefits of open source software are not limited to personal use. Companies and businesses are adhering to the open source paradigm due to the endless possibilities at half the price or lesser.

More and more businesses are converting to open source mainly because it is more cost-efficient than purchasing commercial software. Companies also have more freedom with open source software in terms of customization, since they have the power to mold the software to fit their company's needs. These factors are beneficial in the growth and development of businesses in such a way that the businesses need not to put out a large sum of money just to be able to acquire a software that will be utilized in their business.

Open sourcing has become a way for people to have access to the things that they initially did not have access to. Users of software now have the ability to study the source code of the program they are using, and to know how exactly a certain function of the program runs by looking at its specific line of code.

A sense of community is also created between the software's developers and programmers from outside of their firms. Through open sourcing, the developers are able to communicate with other programmers with regards to how the software can be enhanced further.

Some users would say that using open source operating systems grants more security as compared to paid operating systems. For example, if a user installs the Linux operating system, he or she does not need an antivirus or a virus detection software to keep his or her files intact. The operating system itself has security measures for the user. This becomes a benefit for both professional and nonprofessional users because they have more room for important files rather than installing different kinds of applications for protection.

Open source software is made for the people, by the people. It hones itself to the needs and wants of each user. Because of this, there is no need for the user to upgrade his or her hardware every time the software upgrades.

Take Apple's OSX (operating system) for example. Certain updates of the operating system are available to download, with better features than the previous build. However, older versions of the Macbook and the iMac cannot avail of the recent builds as their hardware are not fit enough to accommodate either the size of the downloaded file or the features itself.

With open source software, the upgrades can be coded to fit each user's needs, depending on the user's hardware. If a certain upstreamed version of the open source software is available to download, different downloaders are made available by the developer with the specifications listed beside each downloader, catering to the different specifications of the user. The user himself can opt to customize the code of the program to be compatible with his device.

Allowing the user these freedoms over the software has given open source software a bit of a leverage over paid, propriety software. But then again, there will be nay-sayers who think that open source software isn't the way to go.

The Downsides and Disadvantages of Open Source

Open sourcing has given users lots of benefits, but it is not perfect. Some would still prefer paid software over any open sourced software. Here are some of the reasons why some users do not approve of open source.

Open Source: Understanding Open Source From the Beginning!

If a user is not in any way a technology expert, he or she would want software that is easy to use. Open source software is known to be more technical compared to their paid counterparts. Paid software focuses on its user interface, making the application easy for the user to understand the system. Open source software usually start out with a not so attractive user interface, but with the basic functions of the program intact. As the program gets updated with each build, the user interface changes and adapts to the needs of its users.

Most critics would say that paid or propriety software is still better in a number of factors as compared to open source software. Because more people are accustomed to using paid or propriety software, the idea that there are other types of software available is intimidating to them. People think that open source software is made only for the technology savvy users, with the interface hard for them to manipulate. Why download a complicated software when they can buy a simple, pre-made software that they are already familiar with?

Paid software has become a norm in the everyday lives of users. Large companies such as Microsoft and Apple have made their name known all throughout the world, creating technologies that users and consumers have grown to love. Because of their undying popularity, the rise of open source software is unknown to the general public. And even if they are known, those who are used to seeing the big names are hesitant to try out what open source might be.

Seeking technical help might seem simple with the numerous open source communities readily available, but it may sometimes be inconvenient to the user. Paid software offer professional tech support straight from the manufacturers.

Chapter 4: The Open Source Culture

Open source gives the user freedom to do whatever he or she wants in a software. Who wouldn't want the freedom to edit source codes to their own liking? With open source, this opportunity of customization is available at hand.

Why are more people converting to open source?

With the source code open for public scrutiny, looking for errors will be easier. Other software companies that do not have their source code publicized have their own set of programmers and developers figuring out the bugs in the software. This is an advantage for companies who always require their software to be updated regularly to keep up with the business.

Students who cannot afford the luxury of paid software turn to their open source counterparts to be able to utilize their functions without having to pay a large amount of money. Open source alternatives of Microsoft Office are available for the students to download should they need to use an office suite for their projects.

Some open source versions of paid software are actually better. Paid media players can play certain file types and extensions, but crash once the file extension is unrecognizable. Open source software developers take note of these bugs and create a media player that can play almost all media file types and extensions in high definition. Because of this, even users who are not actually technology savvy would convert to the open source alternatives of paid software just because they've heard and they know that they can get more out of the open source counterpart.

Programmers who want to practice their coding also rely on readily available open source software in their study. Because the codes of open source can easily be viewed and modified, programmers can base their project on open source software and publish it as their own, creating a program fork.

Businesses, on the other hand, turn to open source software for two main factors: cost efficiency and the power of customization. As mentioned in a previous chapter, with open source software readily available to download on the internet, the businesses do not need to spend a lot of money for a software that they cannot customize as their own. Open source gives them the opportunity to keep on upgrading their system as needed, therefore improving the quality of their software with each build.

The flexibility of open source software has enticed businesses to change to open source from propriety software. Businesses would often buy already existing software and attempt to use them as instructed by the developers. Open source software has its own rules and regulations, but if businesses want their software to be something specific, then the developers of open source software will deliver. With propriety software, the business is the one to adjust to the software that they have purchased, an action that is removed once businesses convert to open source.

Examples of Open Source Software

A wide variety of open source software are available for download. These software may be used for utility purposes, for multimedia purposes – anything that the user desires and requires. Here are a few examples of open source software that you as a user have probably heard of.

The prime example of open source software is an operating system called Linux. It is an operating system based off of UNIX that is available to different computer platforms and hardware.

Another example of open source software is the media player called VLC Media Player developed by the VideoLAN Organization. This media player can run a variety of multimedia files at high definition. Its paid counterpart is Microsoft's own Windows Media Player, which before its most recent build can only play a handful of file extensions.

When it comes to operating systems, Android is another popular example of open source software. A company called Android, Inc. (later bought by Google) has developed this mobile operating system using another open source kernel, Linux. It caters mostly to devices which have touchscreen on them, such as touchscreen desktop monitors, tablets, and smartphones, much like its counterpart from Apple called iOS. Android has its own application store called Google Play, where the users can install applications onto their phones mostly for free.

Netbeans, a well-known software developing application, is also an example of an open source software. It is a Java-created application that caters to different programming languages, and can be run on multiple operating systems. Programmers use Netbeans to create object oriented applications using the 24 programming languages that it caters to.

GIMP, or GNU Image Manipulation Program, is an Adobe Photoshop-like application that edits photos and creates graphic images. It has basic photo editing features such as cropping, grayscaling, and resizing, making it a simpler alternative to Photoshop. Like its paid counterpart, users of GIMP can also create animated GIF images, a feature that most multimedia artists are very fond of using.

Video and computer games can also be open sourced. Some open source games such as Tux Racer are available in the Linux package when downloaded. The principle of open source games is the same as any other open source software – the developers merging and collaborating with the users to create quality content to be distributed to the general public. However, the visual quality and elements of open source games are yet to be improved.

Other examples include PHP (a web development language), MySQL (used in databases alongside applications such as Microsoft Access and Microsoft Visual Basic), Python (programming language), Blender (an Autocad Maya-esque application that caters to 3D rendering), and many more.

Chapter 5: The Future of Open Source

What will happen in the future?

The future of open sourcing seems bright. With most businesses converting to open source software and most developers contributing to open source projects, the growth and expansion of open sourcing will continue. Open sourcing gives way for the innovation of modern software technology – with a lot of people working on one simple open source project, there is no doubt that the project will continue to be updated and improved.

Software will only continue to improve as time passes by. Open source software has made it easier for software to improve and upgrade itself due to countless of volunteers who are up to the challenge. While propriety software claim to start software trends, open source software advocates the upgrades of software that will be favorable to the needs of the users rather than to the bank accounts of the developers.

Open source software does not wish to waste the time and money of the user; rather, it aims to maximize both time and money, with the inclusion of effort, of the user when utilizing the software.

Presently, paid software are still dominant over open source software. Paid software have more leverage compared to open source software when it comes to reliability and familiarity, since they have been used by programmers and users alike for decades. There is still a certain percentage of users who are not aware that there are open source versions of their paid software, which they can help improve and customize to their own needs and liking.

More people will be aware of the benefits of open source software in the future. With propriety software releasing more licenses that restrict its users from certain software freedom, the existence of open source will lead to the users converting from propriety software due to the lack of free will.

In the future, there is a possibility that open source will be available not just for software, but also for other forms of content that have sources.

The future of open source as an idea or a paradigm will not be restricted to software alone. With the further advancement of technology, more and more gadgets will be locked down by licenses and warranties which restrict its users from fixing even simple problems that the product may have.

Gadgets are becoming more and more digitized, and copyright restricts people from ever touching or attempting to change the software. Because of this, some people are beginning to open up to the idea of open source not just for software, but also for hardware and gadgets that are used every day.

Open Source: Understanding Open Source From the Beginning!

Let us take tractors for example. Tractors are machines that are essential in farming. If a tractor breaks down, the farmer himself can fix the broken tractor and keep it running again without having to buy a new one. But the modernization of technology leads the manufacturers of tractors to add digital aspects into their products: tractors now have microchips and are operated via computers, therefore are now protected by copyright.

Now, if the new tractor breaks down, the farmer has no permission to fix the tractor himself. He must hire a specialist to fix the problem, or else he goes to jail.

Open source hardware has already started to rise in its ranks alongside open source software. It basically means that users are free to create their gadgets from scratch, using open source hardware. Although the idea seems taboo at present, the fact that gadgets are also being restricted from the users will give way for both open source hardware and software to rise even further, giving users complete freedom over the creation and implementation of the technology that they need.

Content creators are restricted from creating certain things just because of copyright laws. Even artists, who upload videos on websites like YouTube and Vimeo, get flagged just because of a certain song or a certain speech that had some sort of copyright over it. This restricts creative freedom. It also restricts the content creators from creating what they know and love, and sharing it with their viewers.

Will open sourcing become a culture in the future? Surely, with the massive amounts of information available for the users to share freely amongst themselves. Open source software has given way for an idea that will change the world of computing for everyone, and allows everyone to have access to the large chunk of information that was previously not available to them. Transparency when it comes to creating code and building machines will become a fad in the future, as more and more people are willing and able to create content and share it with other users.

Conclusion

Thank you again for purchasing this book!

I hope this book was able to help you to understand better the concept of open source and its benefits to the public.

Finally, if you enjoyed this book, please take the time to share your thoughts and post a review on Amazon. It'd be greatly appreciated!

Thank you and good luck!

1

www.ingramcontent.com/pod-product-compliance
Lightning Source LLC
Chambersburg PA
CBHW060930050326
40689CB00013B/3039